temp words

alison hart

Copyright © 2014 Alison Hart
ISBN: 978-0-964-5361-4-2
All rights reserved
Second Edition

For my brother Scot and
my mother Mary in spirit land

Contents

temp being

nothing but words 11
cancer 13
embarcadero pier 15
new language 16
pendulum 17
what earth 18
see gulls 19
field 20
eternity 21
grey 22
transcendence 23
sheroes 24
world embrace 26
specks 27
apparition 28
folded napkins 30
flight 34
states 36

temp outrage

noise 39
if Gandhi were a woman 40
gridlock 42
american scheme 43
bush fly 44
angel 45
new orleans 46
how can we hold our sons 50

temp identity

mixed is… 55
some kind of lullaby 56
gathering of self 58
a woman of color 63
talking black to history 65
awake 66

thieves 69
captivity 71
reunion 75
stories 77
what I am and what I am not 79

temptation
half moon 83
friday 84
touch 85
new york joe 86
red ribbons 88
heat 89

temp transcendence
nature 93
smart move 94
drum 96
enough earth 98
tree land 100
redemption 101
myopic topics 102
after the storm 103
laundry mat 104
wind 106
blessing 107
big small 108
transmute 109
I'm going to love you 110
ancient ones 111

ACKNOWLEDGEMENTS

I thank the following for their ongoing support and love: Jerry Thompson, Elaine Dennis, Roberta Tennant, Lisa Terrell, Leslie Hoffman, Janet Hampton, Shawn Terrell, Kate Miller, Tracy Terrell, Danielle Alcala (for the photo!), Gladys Kathman, Barbara Selvidge, Cathy Harrell Kathan, J.C. Johnson, Jody Rich, Espinola Johnson, Jan Goodman, Glenda Mahrus, Susan Jones-Szabo, Jill Walker, Dakota Hoffman, Leslie Hamilton, Tara Yudenfreund, Isabella Nebel, John Terrell, Jo Corpuz, Robin Greenberg, Liz Mcarthy, Victoria Raja, Ricky Ricardo, Jill Carnevali, Olivia Dempster, Laura De La Torre, Joyce Ng, Shawl-Anderson Dance Center (for keeping me sane) and of course my son Luis who inspires me endlessly to be the best soul I can be on this planet,
I love you!

PREFACE

I started writing this book in 1996, when I was working as a temp in San Francisco, mostly as a receptionist. I was grieving the loss of my brother, and took whatever opportunity possible to write underneath the florescent lights. My brother's death rocked my paradigm and forced me to face the temporary reality of our lives. This Buddhist concept of impermanence has liberated me in many ways.

temp words is a journey through impermanence from my perspective as a mixed race woman of color. This is my edge, this is how I navigate through life: one moment at a time.

—a hart

temp being

nothing but words

Searching
the 4 directions
cracked window
opening

leads to the
no where ness
of it all

relive the
pain of the most painful
death
betrayal
of
    new age formulas

chaotic impulses
of the universe
transpire
over any religion

holds nothing but words
laying
empty flat
as stomachs swell
in the eyes of
children
gaping at the
un-realness
of reality

"just chant away the negative energy"

"12 steps"

"jesus"

"guru #"

"tv"

"money"

"meditate"

its all chaos its all chaos its all chaos

"i need a simple answer
so i can live a simple existence"

and why do people that make it seem
self righteous
ego driven
mad
im just jealous
cause im trapped in my life
like a caged bird singing
nameless names singing
nameless
uttered sounds never heard
words scribbled in desperation
before the last cut –

nameless voiceless
nameless formless

I know why the caged bird sings
sings
get me out
     get me out
help me

         get out

cancer

it has taken
my love soul spirit brother
took my grandma
when her hair was still brown
took my uncle before
i could see him
adult eyes to adult
mother's blood brother
cream coffee skin afro –
took
my brother
so young –
suddenly
war in his body
white cells vs. red
no insurance

pneumonia

collapsed lung

breathing machine

not a chance to say
what he felt
  about
      dying before
30.

Capitalism
killed him
     pollutants
white supremacy
             no
health insurance

                poverty
lack of support not
enough earth
to stand on
over concrete he

ran-ran
        up and down
SF hills
        trying
to breathe life
 into his

heart.

a friend now
        suffers to survive
in between chemos
        telling
what life is
        facing
        life
        facing death
i grasp her words
        as if hearing
what my brother could
        not say
with breathing tube
in his mouth –

and i wonder
is it in me
 i wonder –
   and feel the precariousness
of being.

embarcadero pier

Near the crab man
listening for Scot
not having any money
listening.

        Wind, in a dress
feel.

    old. like a
        wise woman
with wrinkled hands and
        soft eyes.

Feather in the sky
    spirit
        flying.

new language

the sun shone on me today
are you part of the sun now?
I want to know you're ok
am I too dense to listen to the dead?

some new language
I must learn

pendulum

Nature took you
is nature cruel or
gentle
was it the answer to
your heavy heart
the vacation you needed?

You stepped over to
the other side & I keep
saying the same thing
over and over

Grief swings
 like a pendulum
till it meets center
and swings again.

what earth

i dyed my hair black
last year
but i didn't know
that was going to be the year
i would lose sight
not able to
see you in the shadow world
you left us for

i gave you my hair
cut it off with the
dust of you
in the dirt
where we grew together
played
you are the earth now
and i
i keep forgetting
what im standing on
 is my own flesh
turned to dust

that year
i dyed my hair black
i didn't know
 it would be the last time
i'd see you
 and i keep looking into the shadows
for answers
black strands pushing out
brown golden light

see gulls

Statuesque

      Guardian of underworld
Twins.

Keepers of

      the sea.

field

today
        pain cleared
with breath
  space
even humor

I see the mountains
I know I have strength
to keep walking

light breeze
over open
field.

eternity

They say
           They say
Death took you away
               from me
but they cant see
        what I see –

no.

Death did not take you

You. No.
It's our little joke
I hear you laughing
           You see me
     smiling

Our little joke.

grey

There are no more
dualities

life is not good
death is not bad

this or
that

that or this –

either or

yes or no

some kind of grey matter

swept up years

centuries of strained

dichotomies

where there are no answers
  because there are no
                        questions.

transcendence

is enough.
the moment of
flight of
belief
catching
a string of hope
amidst
all the breaking
cracking
destruction –
ray of light
breathing in
taking you
to a world
without pain.

sheroes

We were
holding each other up
the three leaning towers
wise women came
to love
even at the hour
of death

one held his body
one held his spirit
one held his heart

and each victory celebrated
strange battle
to be in
watching our loved
one –
surrender
silently gracefully
where we could
no longer see
disappeared into
something unknown –
where he waits for us
when it's
      our time
mother
      lover
sister –
      holding all his
dimensions
      on the path he walked
this time

temp being

loving him till
      very last breath
spilled out
what a strange victory
      love is.

world embrace

Her grace knows
      no corners –
she cant reach –
she holds herself
      high – dignified
blood of royal ones
      whose land we
stand-medicine woman –

My mother
whose face so beautiful
carved over the ages
      of time
her eyes hold the
      sorrow of the
world she tried
to save
Mary. Mary.
it's ok to cry
      to weep
to wail at what loss
 is
Mary it's ok –
      It's ok
and Im loving you
and the world loves
      you back
for what you tried
      to save.

specks

I am filled with the past
of
footsteps
 touching
this pavement
ghosts now

no one knows
 of a soul
who treaded lightly
here

In our own arrogance
we think our lives –
omnipotent
the world begins and ends
with us

so many stories,
lives before us –
we walk in the shadow of.

apparition

Walking to my brother's grave
past farm houses
snowy fields
I step into spirit land
are they resting?

I look for the bench
"We love you mommy"
not Scot's—
recognize the open fields
when we sprinkled his ashes
into a square hole in the earth
trying to joke
saying –
"He'd rather like a circle"
placing my hair –
I cut for him
the last of him
dust
back to the earth
with all these moaning spirits

I find the bench
tears splash
as I dig up the snow
revealing
damp earth
and find his name
1967-1996
so definite
so factual
his life his death

entombed –
under a tree

I light the sage
on the cement plaque
praying to Great Spirit
to the ancestors
I don't ask for anything
but the wind to take
my smoke prayers –
and peace for him
and for him to know
I love him
wherever he is

kneeling in the snow
sage smoke rising
faint wind blows
I empty my thoughts
peace swirls around me
I break off a twig of berries
and place it on his plaque
kiss my finger –
place it on his name
I know he isn't there
that he has become
the sky itself
smiling down
on
me.

folded napkins

"We're busting you out, Mom!"
She spread her arms open.
"Free at last, thank God almighty I'm free at last!"
We all laugh, pile into cars, park in Lexington. We go for a walk, Mom is encircled by us, she, the beginning of us all. She goes with my brother to Peet's to get a cup of green tea. The air is humid, heavy, heavy as the emotions we feel.

She loves walking, can't wait to get away—it is her salvation, movement, being outside with the elements, nature, her religion. What she can't think—we think for her—holding all her memory, maybe she has surrendered it to each of us—each precious moment dropped into our minds, a gift.

We sit under a tree, my brother, sisters, nieces, and my son. My brother takes Mom for a walk. We talk, the children listen.

"Dad wants to take her home."

Her mind spun herself around into a circle of forgetfulness.

"Who took my keys? Where are my keys?"

Forgetting Dad took them so she wouldn't drive, she got lost too many times. Walking to the police station at four in the morning demanding her keys—accusing her granddaughters living in the house, ready for attack on these people that stole from her.
Six times in one week she went walking to the station not remembering she had been before—her mind unraveled, unable to contain itself anymore like neat words on a page like the poetry she wrote.

It screamed sub-text, emotion, dream-like unconscious seeping through her waking state—makes no sense to the rational world we live in. A world of logic time, days, months, years—her mind traveled to a state of being, being in the moment.

Our world has no room for this, no place where the illogical can be—somehow our own need for control wants to shut out the messy possibilities one's wandering mind can bring, the possibilities of metaphors we couldn't understand or emotions we couldn't bear. Swimming in the unconscious is intolerable for us with no way to organize it in neat orderly time boxes.

Is that why we are so frightened of this disease, such a huge threat to our Western cerebral paradigm? I wonder what the ancients did. Maybe they revered the elders with dementia—thought them closer to the spirit world—treated them like shamans, caring for them, making sure of their comfort and needs.

"I'm isolated away from my family. I've been kicked out of my own house…"
"I'm sorry, Mom, I know that's not right."
" Well, maybe I could move back home, but I don't think I want to. It's rather pleasant here, no fighting or yelling. People are very nice here. What should I do, Girls? Should I move back home?"
"No, you're much better living here."
"Okay, well, I suppose you're right, that's settled. I just need my bike and my car but they have no place to put the car, hmm. Have you seen my purse—is it at home?"
"It's in your room, Mom, we'll help you find it."
"Well, okay, I guess I can stay here at this prison. I don't have any money, I am no longer a person, I am a thing."

"I'm sorry, Mom."

"How long am I going to stay here? Do you know how long I'll be here? I'm fine now; I guess it was because I left, I left because I wanted to get out of there. I couldn't take it anymore. I know I can go to California with Lisa—I mean Alison, yes, and find a nice place there, I did that once didn't I and made a nice friend. What was her name?"

"Betty."

"Oh that's right, that's what I'll do, I'll come with you to California."

"Okay, Mom."

We are walking her back to her "apartment" at the assisted living place. The alarm goes off when she enters because she is wearing a GPS device on her wrist in case she manages to "elope" from the building.

"I don't want to stay here anymore, how long have I been here?"

"Oh, maybe a month..."

"Well, that's long enough, time to come home."

"Mom, let's see if lunch is happening."

I bring her over to her lunch table—the distress leaves her face, she sits next to her friend, unfolds her napkin ready to eat. I kiss her but I don't say goodbye, I don't tell her I'm going back to California today—I'm glad she looks peaceful again, at her table with her friends. Ann, a retired High School English teacher, always smiling, making jokes:

"We've been bad, that's why they've put us here, I'm not bad, I've done nothing at all."

"Neither have I and they're just afraid we're going to run away, I mean where are we going to go?" Mom laughs.

"I know." Ann smiles at me. "Can you bring me back some..." (She mimes as if she were taking a drink.) " Just a little one." I laugh, I call them the rowdy table.

Ann says, "Oh, we laugh but that man over there, ooh we

can't laugh next to him, you should see the face he makes, he doesn't like it."

"I don't care, we have a good time." My mom smiles.

I tell my son to go and hug her but not to say goodbye, I watch them embrace, I watch her hold him and whisper gently to him. She sits down and resumes eating. I go back to her room to use the bathroom, tears are welling up, I want to run back to her and hug her, hold her, I burst into tears, touch her bedspread—put my face in her pillow—trying to breathe her in.

"Mommy, Mommy..."

Walking to the elevator I put on my sunglasses—my sister knows I'm crying, she touches my arm. We walk outside; the heavy ornate doors close as thick air encircles us.

"Maybe I could find a place for her—maybe I could."
My sister says gently: "It's okay to cry—just cry." Tears spill out, I hug my son on one side, my sister on the other, my son tries to tickle me so I'll feel better.
"I'll be okay—I'm just sad because I'm leaving my mother."

We walk back to the car. I wonder what we will do without my mother's generation of women, women who are meticulous, careful—who pick up after themselves. Once while visiting at lunch, I watch her friends perform a folding napkin ritual at the end of their meal. "Watch this!" Kathleen demands our attention, thumping her hand on the table, then carefully folds her napkin into a triangle, placing it neatly on the table.

"Oh wait," my mother says, "I can do that. First this corner here then this one."
I watch her fold the corners of her napkin as she gently places it on the table, smoothing it out.
"See, isn't that good?" She smiles, her friends cheer her on.
"Yes, Mary, that's very good."

flight

Mom is gone to the spirit world and I keep saying over and over—she's gone—I think of her words during my last visit at the hospice:

"I'm a wreck."
"Will you please help me get up?"
"Let it go."
"Oh well."
"Will you please help me get up?"

I meditated with her, breathing in calm, out peace. I meditated with my mom, the core of her, calm, but the restlessness, the anxiety let loose like horses running free—unhinged by neo cortex, just out—out.

"Oh Alison, don't let me die here!"

Out, out, sobbing out, I held her, I let her cry, I let her break down. I wish I could have taken her away. My sister held onto her, we all held on to her, we all held on knowing the inevitable. I would leave back to California, my sister would go home to her girls and Mom would stay—listening to:

"Roll out the barrel, we'll have a barrel of fun…" or

"You are my sunshine, my only sunshine…" all the oldies, lyrics still tucked away for her to sing, sing—as she paced down the halls, up and down, back in her chair.

" Will you please help me get up?"

"Will you…"

"No, Mom, it's time to eat, you need to eat first."

"You're mean."

"Yeah, Mom, I'm a mean old teacher."

" Will you please help me get up?"

And she did leave. She left through a window crack—escaped the walls as the oldies songs vibrated in the chests of the residents. She left—as the T.V. blared another old time classic movie—as people paced the halls—moaned, wondering when their time would come—she left—she escaped, all it took was the wind—a tiny crack—an open window.

And she danced on the stars—she hugged the moon—she soared—sending shooting stars for her children to see
she soared
she left
she is free.

states

I am a river of states
bubbling fear
static sadness
frozen rage
rushing sensuality
shimmering joy

I am nature
the constant change
of the sky
the unforgiveable
impermanence
a temp on this earth
a tiny imprint
of sound with
each step.

temp outrage

noise

love is not silent

it rages
           screams
cries   laughs

but is it ever silent
      not feeling anything?

hate
with its explosive nature
destroys

where love
 coming from the same vortex
          creates

it is never silent
      and in my anger
I know love
In my many shades of feeling
       I know love
and it may scream through me
cry through me sing through me
whisper through me
but no, no,
it is never silent.

if Gandhi were a woman….

"Oh beautiful
  Oh spacious skies
blah blah blah blah
         blah blah
Oh purple mountain–"

Look at that brown
woman going hungry
Do you see
     Gandhi in her eyes
as she proudly
       walks down
the street in a
   spaced out glance
saying
     Hunger

"blah blah blah fruited plains
America   America"

Could you spare some
change could you –

I wonder if Gandhi were a woman
and starved herself
would people care as much –

some change please?

"blah blah blah blah
on me–"

temp outrage

who cares about the brown woman
doing her hunger walks
the black woman with the cup in her hand
 the white woman selling her body for
"America America—"

And I wonder if Gandhi were a woman —
people would even care at all
 at all

"From sea to —

and one thing a woman can never be is

too rich or too thin
too rich or too —

"shining sea—"

gridlock

Step
between the cracks
Iron gates
	lock at your ankles
If you cant move –
quick enough
Massive Modern Gridlock

SNAP

feet are gone
cant get up

SNAP

legs –

SNAP SNAP SNAP

left with a paper cup
jingling change

"Please cant you help me?"

You're not moving fast enough
no one stops
afraid of the
	dismemberment

have to keep up the pace
in this concrete mistake

Survival dance
of the fittest

Capitalist   delusions

american scheme

Genocide dream
blood stained earth
at what cost

a building
       a house

the ancestors
       bones rattle
in warpath

              rage

what dream —

shackled to shopping carts
pushing ahead
         ahead to —

what dream?

How can a dream be made on genocide

what dream —
      are you talking about
with no conscience

bush fly

I had a dream
I was in a room full of protesters
Bush came down the aisle
shaking hands

I went to shake his hand
I realized how short he was

I said

 Maybe you should have been an actor and I should have been a politician because I would do a much better job than you!

He laughs and says

You have no idea

Then I went off on him

No more war in Iraq – how can you let them fight there- they are babies babies – coming home with no limbs – no limbs –
no arms legs
What is their life gonna look like –
How can you make them go?
They're babies
babies!!!

I was screaming at him so hard
he turned into a small fly and hid up by the rafters
hovering
in a corner.

angel
(dedicated to Garret Paul Johnson)

Who held you that night
screaming
to a heaven

Who

You young beautiful
man
       Beautiful –

What year is it?
       Burning crosses

       What year?

Rights of Civility
  ravaged
           what year?

When will white men
    Stop perpetrating
unlawful nature saga of torture

Who
       Who held you that night
screaming
      to a heaven
          unheard

new orleans

Tank trucks with armed soldiers
people –
stranded in disarray
babies –
look questioningly to the camera
why –
where is their food
and whose child's tummy is hungry
heart scared
are they with their mommy and daddy?

Are the children saved-where do they go for
comfort –
they are not refugees
they are Americans

refugee: "a person who flees from his home or country
to seek refuge elsewhere as in a time or war, political
or religious persecution..."

Americans
they live here they belong here
America looks watches
just black people
those aren't really Americans –
I wonder does Condy Rice shed a tear
or does she see these people as low black vs.
hi black –
no bus ticket no place to go
up up up on a roof
and wait wait it out
in attics wait

for someone to notice
their own humanity enough to do something –

Shoot the looters
Shoot the looters
Shoot the –

You know that if they were white the whole picture
would be different
You know that if it were rich white people's homes
things would be different
Shoot to kill

I got to get some bread for
my baby
my baby

Shoot!

There is a war going on
and it's in our backyard –
but I don't hear enough about it
not like the tsunami which sprung immediate action

What have we done
do we really have no soul no
conscience no
caring – no –
the lowest of low
cant we see our eyes in theirs
cant we –
this 2005 not 1865
slavery is abolished –
all men created equal –
to sit and wait

while babies tummies ache
older people
limp in hospital chairs
to sit and wait –
for what
for what
so when people look for food
Shoot to kill!

Disbelief, I see in their faces
that they are being treated this way
utter disbelief
and rage –
and I wonder –
what will stem from this seed of
disaster
dis-concern

What it stirs
in the have nots
of this country –
being so
disregarded lives not counted
tossed to the side like
this can wait –
this can wait while
Cindy Sheehan
waits and waits
mothers asking
why
why –
did my baby die

What for

temp outrage

Same look
same questioning
eyes as
hungry children
stare at camera
in New Orleans
the city of people –
of any city
any people –
when will
the questions be answered
and if not answered
with what
force of rage grief will explode onto the conscience
of the have haves
in America
into their lives –

and I see a war coming – I see it
I see it coming

how can we hold our sons

If walking down the street
going to the store
taking public transportation
being in the world is a threat
demonized for their color
seen as a predator to be
preyed upon

When happy trigger
racists
are empowered to
take the law in
their own hands

When there is no justice
their lives seen as
meaningless insignificant
disposable
amidst a modern day lynching
epidemic

history rears its ugly head
Billie Holiday's
"Strange Fruit"
echoes in the ears of protestors
I AM A MAN
I AM A MAN
I AM A MAN
I AM HUMAN
Not some picnic lynching
party amusement
human equal human

temp outrage

How can we hold our sons in this world
in this world
our sons my son
your son
How can we hold them?
Tell me how?

temp identity

mixed is…

Holding the illusion of race
being an embodiment of enemies
a vessel to hold the tension of dualism
created by racism.

Wanting to be lighter
wanting to be darker
wanting straight hair
wanting curly hair

being a bridge for everybody else

looking for a bridge for yourself

being your own bridge

loving yourself
hating yourself

being a Buddhist

waving no flag.

some kind of lullaby

Helen
Grandmother Helen
wanted to be a singer
and sang
in Old Orchard Beach Maine
with one of the greats
Calloway?
Ellington?
but she didn't want to go on tour

her tight lipped mother
Emma
black Indian soul
kicked off reservation?
brown/black skin
betrayal?

and through those tight lips
did notes flow to your ears
like some kind of lullaby
Helen?

when you stopped
singing did
drunkenness soothe
your dreams
dulled into
nightmares violence?
Did it?
   Did it?

Did Mary's cries
stop you stop you

temp identity

from one last
hit

And Mary's voice
soothe her child
self to sleep –

and sing to me
her child
with almond eyes
to calm my dreams
my dreams –
weaving into
some kind of lullaby
        some kind

gathering of self

It's New Year's Eve– I'm waitressing at "La Brasserie" in Embarcadero 3, San Francisco, trying desperately not to strain my back, show my vulnerability, and keep my humor going while balancing hot plates on my arms. Not an easy task, especially when customers are tipping ten percent. Do they detect my insides? My great acting ability is failing me tonight? And so here I am waiting. Waiting, still waiting, waiting for a kind remark, a human connection, a nice tip– a laugh, a look– a –

I look over to the owner, Richard, and his woman "Du jour." She is maybe twenty years old, with long swept hair. Richard is a French man I feel sorry for, especially when he dances; he tries to look so cool and all I can do is laugh or feel pity. The man has very little soul. But nevertheless he is the owner, the big cheese, the –

He looks like her father, they throw glances at each other from across the table, he gently strokes her white carved face as her expression remains the same, a smile or a pout probably well rehearsed from studying magazines and looking in the mirror. She, dressed in black, sits elegantly while he dotes on her every desire.

Meanwhile, I am clearing the plates off a table. I try not to strain my back as I head towards the bus station. Somehow I long for my long hair again, decide to grow it. I look over to their table, they are engrossed in each other's roles. I can hear what he's saying-I know her response, I feel like I'm watching a bad T. V. show and then I realize I'm in one— the restaurant business. Oh yeah. Forgot this wasn't reality. But something jabs my insides–

"You're nothing, just a low down waitress, nobody servant ugly wretched unloved being that will never get anywhere."

I exhale– try to regain composure and check on my party

of seven. They want more drinks and want to know when the dancing will start. The father of this family looks disapprovingly towards me— demanding that I find out when the music will come on. I try to make a joke, his sternness will not move. I start to feel like nobody. I look over at Richard's table. I feel worse, see, she's somebody, I'm nobody. She gets to sit there while I have to deal with asshole customers— and a bad back.

There is something wrong with this picture. Why am I envious of her— me— that would never ever think of playing that princess from hell role again, exorcised it out of me or —
have I really.
I am ashamed of my feelings that I envy her bad acting job, that I envy her being taken care of, being special, being adorned —
being —

Time to fire table ten— I try not to think about it— exhale— joke with the wait staff. I'm getting old, that's it and I'm losing my chance for love so I better grow my hair and start pouting again so I won't lose my chance for love. But I know it's not love, it is a lie— that I've known— that I became once— not love.

But the question is— who is having more fun?

I stop to chat with Richard, one of the waiters, not to be confused with Richard the owner (pronounced Ri-shard, very chic and French). We have a chat in front of the men's bathroom.

"So Richard, gee I wonder what I'll be doing in 1993? Maybe I'll start a new career or gee maybe I'll be taking an order or clearing a table—" I laugh mockingly to him.

"You can be sure," he says, enjoying my humor, "you will not be a high sky diver so— that career choice can be eliminated."

"Oh yeah gee, I know maybe I'll end up being a waitress in 1993!"

"Well, I think I know what's going to happen to you in '93."
"Oh yeah?"
"Oh yes. I'm right about these kind of things." He looks at me, tilting his head; somehow I feel he does know something– a perfect father figure for me, curly black hair, distinguished beard, glasses, Richard, always ready to engage in something witty, intelligent and not afraid to mock himself– yes, he must know something.

"Oh really," I say intrigued with his remark. "What?"

He pauses a moment then in his very Richard-like fashion speaks rapidly with such knowingness that anyone would believe him:

"You see, you're going to be walking down the street going about your business, or you'll walk into some place, just then you'll see someone, your eyes will meet and it will happen, this energy between you, you'll fall in love." He stopped. I blushed and tried to make levity of his premonition.

"Well, ha. God help me."

"No, no, God help him," he answers with a big smile.

"God help us both." I laugh and Richard goes about his duties. I leave feeling that something sweet was given to me– that I had gotten my New Year's present. Maybe he was right. Maybe Richard has super human intelligence, maybe –

Well, it certainly helped me get through the rest of the night.

It's almost twelve, the DJ's blasting "Love Shack" from the B-52's. I order champagne for a table– the crowd shouts the countdown– everyone is wearing party hats, tiaras, blowing horns. I have a tiara on while placing the glasses of champagne on a table. I blow my horn– it's 1993– I grab the empty glasses from the table and bring them to the bus station. I sing loud as I walk through the crowd, dancing to the beat. The bartenders Lynn and Patty are grooving in synch with tiaras and blowing horns.

I pass Richard (the waiter), he stops. "Happy New Year,

sweetie," he says and kisses me, I kiss him back and say, "Happy New Year." I look over to Richard's table (the owner). During the last few seconds of 1992, they look into each other's eyes and kiss, a completely contrived moment, something I wouldn't have done in high school. I laugh. I laugh to myself thinking of my envy of their unreality. Laugh.

Oh well, fuck it, I say to myself- Patty, knowing I don't drink, pours me 7-up in a champagne glass, we toast to the New Year. Streamers are thrown in the air, clinking of glasses heard in between shouting, laughter. But I want to get out of there, out of this unreality. I want to meditate on my experiences of the past year– have a moment of my reality– ha– that's what poverty is– always serving some one else's dream while you barely have time for your own.

I walk out, but I am stopped by Bernard, the very sly, trying to be sexy, married French Manager. "Have you cleared your tables?"

"Yes," I lie.

"Okay."

He looks at me blankly while I turn to leave. It's raining, I put my scarf over my head and keep saying over and over to myself, I am centered, no matter what happens around me, I am centered. Something is choking around my neck. I need to cry?

Somehow saying no to the old ways, saying goodbye to the old me is harder than actually participating in the B.S. When I do that, I know what the outcome will be– I know what taste it will leave, I have grown accustomed to the bitterness.

I walk down the street to Bart, raindrops plunking down– a group of drunk people pass me –

"Happy New Year, sweetie!" they shout.

"Happy New Year," I say, only because I thought they would get hostile if I didn't. "Crazy drunken people," I whisper to myself. I head down the stairs to the train. The Bart comes quickly enough and then the 22 Fillmore comes miraculously soon too. I'm walking the four blocks to my apartment on Bryant Street; the rain is getting more serious. I start laughing then singing so loud, the rain dances on the pavement, I sing louder. A car passes, a man asks me if I want a lift, I say no.

"Come on, baby, why not?"
"I like the rain."
"What?"
"Me gusta el lluvia."
"Come on, why not?"
"I'm fucking crazy!"

Then I start to laugh and sing more– he drives away. A baptism into 1993, I sing so loud I hit high notes that pierce through the wind and rain– the rain acts as percussion– halleluiah– I sing as I approach my apartment –

HALLELUIAH –

I get into my apartment, out of wet clothes and light a candle for the New Year. I know I'm doing the right thing, I know it, I think to myself as I make some tea. Living a life of integrity is the only way, building the house within. I know it. Somewhere tears come– the old ways– the old pain– the old making way for the new, the newer, the unknown, exhaustion overcomes my limbs– I walk into my room, blow out the candle and let sleep take me over.

a woman of color

How long has it been
that I've hid my own skin
a woman of color
too many hands
passed over my flesh
to pass some white test
caught in a dream
living out lies
for someone else's needs

I cry
who am I
pretty young thing?
accept the beauty within
not cover my skin

You look at me with uncertain eyes
hiding disgust
"how could she, how could she
be so mixed up"
"What are you what are you," as you crinkle your nose,
"What are you what are you –
not pure white I suppose."
"Look at me look at m e
in a magazine –
my hair is so pretty my skin
so clean so clean.
There's nothing wrong with me
Im pretty don't you see
Im pretty Im pretty
pretty is me.
What school did you go to?

where do you live
your color annoys me –

but I guess I'll forgive
I'll pretend I don't see her
she'll never know she can't read my thoughts
I won't let them show.
What color is she –
can I trust her dark skin?
Or maybe it's just a tan or
something.
Not pure like mine
no, pure as white snow
not pure like mine –
I'm much better I know.
SHHHHHHHHHHH!
Maybe she'll hear
words will leak through my ear
but she's white enough white enough
she's white enough to be here."

talking black to history

I will not be your
tragic mulatto
quadroon octoroon
bi racial tri racial
caught between your race wars
as if all race is
black & white
 slit wrist of societal hatred of itself
atomic explosions of
differences
in one cell
    one body
     one mind

I will not be your
tragic mulatto
to satisfy your need for
affirmation
"See that doesn't work"
or climb out of
my skin
to fit into
your hate suit –
whatever color

I will not be your
tragic mulatto
high yellow seductress
exotic hybrid
sexual
fascination
my back
the bridge
carrying your weaknesses
I carry my own weight
not yours– there's nothing tragic about me.

awake

They took us

e x t e r m i n a t e d

families
with gifts of
infected pox blankets

made us
"the savages"

them "the noble white people"
trying to help the
poor misguided brown savages

Forcing the cross
on our babies
taken away from families
colonized minds
puppets to christian ideas
native tongue
cut out by beatings

We learned to see our skin
language
culture
as bad
to be beaten out of us –
until completely
forgotten –
only remembered in
dream states

living off
reservation

in victorian home
teased for their brown skin
features

Dream states

Who am I?

internalized racism
century grown hatred
in stomachs of ancestors
passed on
disguised as
alcoholism, drug abuse

We lost our words
replaced with
our father's
mumbled prayers
on rosary beads

We accepted the hatred
and sought
to become like their
tribe
white privileged important
their tribe
entitled

We put our worth in their hands
longing
for acceptance
we erased ourselves
lost to the pages of history books
as the good indians giving food
on thanksgiving

Our dream states
trying to wake us
up to who we were
trying until —
someone breaks apart with
self hatred
disguised as alcoholism drug abuse suicide
until someone screams
WHO AM I
in this white washed world
until someone acknowledges their
self hatred and dares to look at it
discover its origins

and we are brought back
to the beginning
of an innocent mind
whose worth was
self evident
independent from
another's gaze

back to unfamiliar sounds

Spasu qey tankahk*
(awake hello how are you)

as nature intended us to be

*Passamoquoddy language

thieves

Sometimes
I can't find my words –
I have no words
they are stuck
somewhere
deep
in me
sounds
  I've never
heard
  rhythms
caught
  somewhere
in my back –
deep –

Sometimes –
I have
no words –
to get to them –
painful
  tearing
of loss
  grief
what happened
babies torn
from mothers
cultures torn
from
communities
left naked –

Where are my words?

I try to find them
in rhythms in movements
in songs –

Where are they

Who
   Stole

      Them?

(Culture isn't as easy as putting on some cowry beads or lighting some sage– we have to look to history– reveal its painful past, that is our only access– through pain)

captivity

Held in his gaze
brownwhiteblack woman
survivor
      replaying old
tapes of history

"He won't leave me, he
will provide for me…"

The mother cries at the wedding

His ancestor's need
For control –
      The ultimate
control over another
slavery –
2 generations earlier
in the south –
his great granddaddy was –

"Good to them, let them stay on the plantation
after emancipation –
cause they had no where else to go."

Good to them
owned them beat them
squeezed a livelihood
out of them –
      but
  was good to
them –
      them –
not people or animals
maybe something
in between
      them
he married one of

        them
a light skinned
        them
an educated them
from Maine

His parents didn't go to the wedding

Her father
black business man
left her mother
irish/indian/black
to raise her children
while she drank
        and beat them
her father –
who loved his little girl
left them
        little girl
a mother already at 5 –

He remarried
and visited sometimes
to play jazz by ear on the piano

History repeated itself
it's old tapes
laws never erased
implanted in the blood
of descendants of enslaved/enslavers
the marriage vows
        the wedding cake
the mother's tears

"I don't think you should marry him…"

I do

temp identity

      I do

Held her in bondage
in fear
      captive again

The ancestors groan

Babies are born
not black not white not Indian
a swirl of color
in between

His fear holds
      them
his anger
      tears
into their flesh
they carry it for
      him

She doesn't
      leave
she feels enslaved
5 babies
      Where to go?
Where do we
      go –
no where else to go

Children leave
grow up
world perpetrates
on them –
they take it in their bodies
trying to tear away
the chains of the past –
      echo of their father's screams

One
the last child
doesn't make it
too much painangerhostility
to see
endure
poisons his blood –
leukemia
takes him
his spirit soars to the sky –
the eagle takes him
to the ancestors
and as he watches
grandchildren are born
the next generation
trying not to forget history
to not repeat it

The house closes in
on silence
       now
she, held still
no longer taking it in
       the rage
of his generations

She waits in quiet
       Listening
to his footsteps
       echo –
on the stairs

She knows
       It
is
       time to
             go.

reunion

the land accepted us
wasn't weighed down by our
ambiguous colors
olive brown black white
beige skin

golden curly straight brown
black frizzy hair

it didn't question us
ask us to choose sides
black or white
as if they were the
only two to choose from

we could stand whole
connected
to each other
without suspicious
glances –
or looks like

"you just don't belong here"

or

"I couldn't tell you were black"

brown, gold, black, white
hands meet
"I'm your cousin..."
no room for racism here
"I'm your Aunt, Uncle..."

fragments of America –
the real America
that no one wants to see

check a box
choose a side
but don't acknowledge the
mixture

we cannot separate
ourselves from history
history from ourselves

seeds burgeoning from the
earth we stand
stories begging
to be told

stories

Survived my own story
stories running thru
my veins
my own –
 ancestors –

running
running through
woods
someone falls on
the trail
too late they
shot her
leaves brown –
trees– sunlight
fear –
running thru my veins
stories –
I survived my own –
my ancestors survived theirs
now lodged in my back –
memories
waiting for the words
images
sound –
breath –
giving new life
to old
trauma traumas
traumas
how old

escaping thru the underground
railroad-running
running-escaping
from
potato famine
surviving squalor of
ships diseases
dysentery typhus –

serfs
thrown off their land
in Scotland
settling in the south
one English officer
coming to America

Stories intermingle
contradict –
asking to be found –
an opening somewhere
stories
waiting for breath
light
exhumed
from tight lipped ancestors
staring back at me
Let me hear them speak.

what I am and what I am not
(or what I can take to the grave and what I cant)

I am not my car
I am not my home
I am not my age
I am not my phone

I am not my clothes
I am not my face
I am not my job
I am not my race

I am not my hair
I am not my shoes
I am not my spouse
I am not my blues

I am
     the poem waiting to be written
the space
       in between words
the dance
       waiting to be moved

I am not a corporation
a symbol of any status
if you look at me
you cant see me
there are no labels
you wont find me
like sand slipping through
your fingers
meaning is gone

I have carved out
my own space
and I sing
      my own
           song

temptation

half moon

ladies. bursting in want
out of their clothes
tight
see my body?
burning
seeking yearning for
something like the moon
soothing –
     inviting –
someone grabs her hand –
pulsing
to the beat
endless-endless
as all our own heart beats –
beat –

catching a glance
he lights a cigarette
is this the one?
the one?

outside the moon
in half yellow perfection
waits to be found
by empty longing.

friday

Missing
your strong arms
around me
like a circle of light
                        breath
in our home
    between
                each other
as you walk
calmly
in the midst of chaos
and I
scramble time
for poetry
under fluorescent lights
constant buzz
            watching
the clock.

touch

im afraid
that my love for you will explode in gallop
like one of Joy Harjo's
horses
wild relentless demanding
im pouring
my self into your arms hand eyes
terrified
at what I've done
I long to pull the reins tight
come to a halt
in the safety of a wall
this wild horse
breaks free
and I hope I wont
fall
too hard

new york joe

now
let me hold your thigh
don't you like this?
              ooooh softer
                    now –
why don't you like my kisses –
here look
we can do this –
now kiss me– let me pull you
closer

Do you want to sleep over?
no– just sleep –
           I promise –
now– look at this
we can do this

What do you want for christmas,
it's no big deal
here, you know
I'm a nice guy –
          right –
let me pull you closer –
has anyone told you about
your eyes?
anyone said they're
            pure –
                    mysterious –
huh? No?
     What's wrong with them?
Can't I have a hello kiss –
     that's nice
you look beautiful

        no– I mean it
you look beautiful –
I bet you hear that all the time –
I like your hair
            this is the first time
I've seen it,
Can I touch it –
        oh yeah –
beautiful.
yeah. Lets do this –
      you don't have any money
a little?
Ooooh come here –
does this tickle
      huh?
So –
      are you coming home with me tonight?
Huh?

red ribbons

Is your love
in the fast lane
like the cars you drive
the women you've
had
who you say you didn't love
as you love me.

I give myself to you –
over and over
and I watch you
take me in you
holding your limp body like
a baby resting his head on my breast.

There isn't any more I can give you
I unravel myself
red ribbons
as you pull me nearer
"are you mine"
you say –
I don't understand
all I've been is with you –

I hold my breath
when you leave at night
hoping Im not the other women
who in my dreams
tell me to be weary
clutching cigarettes
and sipping wine

heat

you stay with me
whether I want you to
or not
all the touching
exploring fumbling
dance 24 hours
walk break drama break
movie break
and then
we inhale
each other again
as if for the first time
tongues lips
skin to skin
on fire –
and I am consumed
and not consumed
and I see the warning signs
yet I still
can
        not
stop

temp transcendence

nature

Blue nature
Flew nature
Do nature
Few nature
View nature
Goo nature
Zoo nature
Hue nature
Cue nature
You nature
You

                        nature

smart move

time taken from me
body explosions
of
what was done
pre verbal me
soaked up the rage
soaked up the pain
soaked up the blame

I became blame
and wore guilt
on my face –
in my breath
in my body –

I became rage
and watched it
explode from my limbs
to my fingertips
        O U T
leaving me in
lumps
on the floor
leaving me
s p l i n t e r e d
from my self
true self

I became the hurt
    enough time
taken away from me
enough years
swimming on

temp transcendence

land —
just keeping
nose above the water
just enough —

What is left
can be left to
imagination
  creation
I will move it
it will not
move me —
I will take it
in my breath
and release
exhale —
no longer tormentor
no longer victim

I am living

        I am alive

drum

I reach past generations
past the learned shame
self hate
brought upon by foreigners

I reach past the waters they dove into
freedom
from forced enslavement

I reach past
the chiseled off
reservations
a fragment of the earth
they called home

I reach past
the tears of culture
buried in graves
of the ancestors lips
shut tight
no more secrets let out
to survive became to forget

I reach past the learned self hatred of
their skin
brown-black
as
less other ugly

I reach past forgotten words
languages

In the pulse of the drum

something comes back to me –
my pelvis opens
my spine expands
the beat brings me
back
to the heart of my ancestors
the wise ones –
who never learned
shame
I peel back the layers of
self hatred, self denial
I take pleasure in my body
this flesh –

I reach back
I peel away
I reach back
I peel away
I feel my heart beat
the sage smoke rises –
the wind takes it.
They hear my prayers.

enough earth

is there enough earth
to hold all our dreams?
or
is time running out
as glaciers melt and
carbon rises

is there enough earth to hold all our dreams?
or
are slides quakes tsunamis
triggering
flight fright freeze
lower brainstems activate
ready to run

is there enough earth for all our dreams?
or
did this generation use it up
feeding banks while children's mouths
hang open

is there enough earth to hold all our dreams?
or
do they only exist at night
causing no waste
no heavy steps
no need to worry about tomorrow
or the next ten years
when climate change
is irreversible

is there enough earth to hold all our dreams?
if I could

temp transcendence

I would hold yours in my hand
little one
tell you not to worry
go run
go play
Im holding it
      holding it
           for you.

tree land

my spirit knows
the body goes
death will leave it
over exposed
mind will stop
heart will cease
but spirit will drift
to a higher peace.

Im no body
to be used
in your chain of abused
those that do
know too well
the price too high
the cost to sell.

take my fragile framework of
body made of flesh and blood
let me see beyond my self
and travel with those
that do without.

speak to me
oh light above
let me breathe
into your love
leave behind the shallow past
move on to stronger love that lasts.

redemption

One of those nights
im gonna remember
when the sky was just so –
and people came
hanging
with all their funkiness
even the trees were dancing
as the music rang
and the wind answered
explosion of souls flying

The Cherokee brotha
chanting
        for our grief
African brothas
chanting
        for our joy
cradled us as
drummers drummed
for the prayers to be sent
dancers danced
for freedom

The ancestors
watched in shock, reverence
"How did all these people come together?"
all races
all ages
 weaving
a new beginning

myopic topics

race
just another ploy
to convince us of the illusion
of separateness

sex
just another ploy
to convince us of the illusion
of separateness

the illusion
that we feel
greater or lesser than

a tree
        a rock

spirit
connects us in death/life
spirit connects.

after the storm

In my own castle
of words
····colors thoughts in
magenta
gifts of flowers

peace
················is
hard earned

laundry mat

Maybe it was
the way the sun hit
the window at
that certain time of
day when
evening creeps in on us
before the pink moment
of sunset

or
the lullaby hum of the driers

I felt my soul in this
laundry mat this
laundry mat in Oakland
where America has
decided it's ok
to hang out
and wash
wash your clothes
this is the place
America
      washes her clothes
the dirty laundry
to come get clean

And one woman
her shiny face
gray hair
walking with a cane
her expression remains in constant
dialogue

temp transcendence

washing drying
TV blaring
      man reading next to me
10 hot minutes for 25 cents

There is beauty everywhere
her smile says –

in every moment
          god is.

wind

I exist in flight
my only name
gravity
the only constant
flight
open arms
deep breath
bird song
belonging to nothing
but the wind

blessing

to crack
and let unknown
rivers
break the
dam
    of my
bitterness

reach out for your
hand and
be able to begin
again –
something I can carry in my heart
always

big small

I've gone deeper
in my realization of
why I'm here and
what I'm doing
I feel
lately when I'm singing
I'm not singing or
I feel like I'm just breathing
it feels –
simple
like pouring water
out of a vessel

nothing big

and in the smallness
      of my
being
I am big

and in the bigness of my being
small

all I aspire to is to heal –
and share the healing –
in small ways –
which are
big.

transmute

like the snake
shedding skin
finding new
state of grace
to be in
becoming the
answers
instead of
living the questions
releasing the pain
instead of creating
new lessons.

I'm going to love you

no matter
who you are
any color
size
s e x u a l
orientation

I'm going to love you –

so watch out
watch out
w/your
h a t r e d

Love is
here!

ancient ones

I feel them
all around me
in me
with me
guiding me
protecting me
teaching me
their silent ways
my heart
is broken
they know
theirs were too
they know
what land was stolen from their bodies
I feel them
asking me to listen
beyond words

www.ingramcontent.com/pod-product-compliance
Lightning Source LLC
Chambersburg PA
CBHW030447300426
44112CB00009B/1201